I0571633

Grid Liberation

Take Control of Your Electricity — The Currency
of the New World

By Brett Joerger

Copyright © 2024 by Brett Joerger

All rights reserved. No part of this book may be used or reproduced by
any means, graphic, electronic, or mechanical, including photocopying,
recording, taping, or by any information storage retrieval system, without
the written permission of the publisher except in the case of brief
quotations embodied in critical articles and reviews.

Dedication

"This book is dedicated to my mother, Tricia Joerger, for her unwavering love and support. As a single mother, she taught me strength, resilience, and the power of hard work. She is my rock and my guiding light. Thank you for raising me to be the person I am today. This book is a testament to the incredible power of motherhood and the impact a mother's love can have on a child's life."

Contents

Foreword

It is my pleasure to write the Foreword for "Grid Liberation" by Brett Joerger. As his number two in command, I have had the privilege of working closely with Brett and witnessing his passion and dedication to harnessing the power of the sun for the benefit of all. Brett's vision and leadership is what carries everyone through. He can motivate and inspire in the darkest of times and he does it repeatedly.

But it is not just Brett's technical expertise that makes this book a must-read. It is his ability to inspire and lead others that truly sets him apart. He is a true leader and I am honored to work by his side.

In "Grid Liberation," Brett shares not only his technical knowledge, but also the inspiration and motivation that drives him to make a difference. He shows how anyone can make a difference in the world and how everyone can benefit from sustainable energy solutions. I highly recommend this book to anyone who wants to learn more about sustainable energy solutions and how they can make a difference in the world.

—Akash Singh

Introduction

"Never give up trying to build the world you can see, even if others can't see it."

—Simon Sinek (British-American author and motivational speaker)

It was Friday the 13th of March 2020. An ominous sign? Perhaps. But no werewolves were howling and no hockey-mask-wearing supernatural killers were on the loose. On this particular evening, nothing but good vibes and positivity filled the air at the corporate headquarters of Westhaven Power in Yuba City, California.

As the company's Chief Executive Officer (CEO), I decided it was time to recognize the amazing group of individuals who had been helping to build a company from humble beginnings (my garage) to one generating over $30 million in revenue.

Our performance was at an all-time high, with every department firing on all cylinders. Salespeople, installers, and everyone else in the company were having a positive impact on our collective mission to provide solar energy solutions to as many people as possible. Team morale was also clicking, as everybody was working together to create something special; it was definitely time to celebrate.

A party of that magnitude required the room and food to match the exuberance of its message. To do this the right way, we cleared out any clutter in our celebration room, a renovated 4,000-square-foot space where we gather for meetings, conferences, and events. It features an eighteen-foot door that rolls up (similar to a loading dock door), making it a unique environment to allow sunshine, fresh air, and blue skies to penetrate the surrounding walls.

The food? We partnered with a local pizza shop to have it catered. This was no ordinary pizza delivery, though. We didn't simply have a college kid in a 1986 Toyota Camry with a glowing advertisement for Joe's Pizza on its roof deliver twenty-five cheese pizzas. Instead, we enlisted the services of a five-star local pizza shop named Rolling Stone Pizza. They showed up with a woodfired pizza baking trailer! No grease-stained cardboard boxes to dispose of and no antacid needed; just on-demand gourmet pizza for everybody.

Within about fifteen minutes of our designated party time of 3:00 pm, employees had begun filling the room, along with the aroma of fresh-baked pizza and the springtime air. People were mingling, eating pizza, and partaking in the day's festive mood. All was right in the world at Westhaven Power, as everyone awaited a message from their leadership.

I stepped onto the stage and told everyone how much I appreciated their expertise and amazing all-around contributions to the company. We had achieved a level of success I hadn't imagined when building state-of-the-art devices to harness solar power in the garage of my home twelve years prior.

"We are the apex of our ancestors," I began. (I always preferred to honor those that went before us to get us here) I continued, "As such, we have the responsibility to deliver resources to the maximum of our capabilities. The sacrifices made by our predecessors to get us to this point in our evolution are far greater than anything we face today. Thank you for your commitment to our cause, the dedication to your work, and your contributions to our mission for grid liberation!"

The commencement of speeches from a few other company leaders was met with sustained energy and confidence from the crowd. There were even a few thunderous rounds of applause and a standing ovation or two. For the next few hours, everyone felt like they were part of a company on a meteoric rise. We were all in the right place at the right time. Then, the world turned upside down.

Chaos Crashes the Party

Several months prior to that celebration day, I had heard rumblings about a new virus. My wife is a physician and had been tracking COVID-19 since the start of the new year. All we knew was that China was having a hard time controlling it (at least from what leaked in the media). When they shut things down over there, she became rightfully concerned. However, I still hadn't given it much thought until the next shoe dropped.

When Italy told everyone to stay home, the repercussions of a pandemic became a reality for me. Before that, I figured that the story in China may have been some dark fairy tale that would never come to fruition anywhere else. I'm half-Italian and have been to Italy, so them shutting down made COVID start to seem real for me. At that point, I thought, "Imagine what it would be like for a business owner to be told they have to shut down? What would happen to the workers? The customers? The company? What would happen to the country?" I thought, "Whew, thank God it's still happening an ocean away from us."

If only that were true. As everyone knows, COVID-19 was already spreading in the United States. The majority of the population (including myself) had no idea of its implications yet. Soon enough, large events began shutting down. "That doesn't sound good," I thought. Then, the news came from our federal government that all non-essential businesses were to cease operations. "China, Italy, and the U.S. What's going to happen next?" I thought. Chaos had officially crashed our party at Westhaven Power and around the world.

Unfortunately, nobody had yet written the *Business Leader's Survivor's Guide to Pandemic Shutdown,* so there was no precedent about what to do. There was no case study to research—no *in case of emergency, break glass* tool to reach for and lead everyone down a virtual fire escape to safety. Business leaders worldwide had no idea what to do next, nobody did.

Now what? Panic? That's never a solution to anything, but the leadership team at our company took a few minutes to soak in the news. Then, we had to come up with a plan.

Fortunately, because we were a power company, we were deemed *essential.* My first thought was, "Great!" Then I wondered, "Well, what does that mean?"

It turns out that being deemed essential meant we could continue operations, but we could not go inside people's homes to sell our solar systems. In other words, our ability to generate revenue was mostly gone.

When revenue is stripped to almost nothing, costs need to match it. That meant we had to stop payments for human capital. Sadly, we had to furlough about 90 percent of the workforce. We went from a company of 130 proud, hard-working, and damned good people to a skeleton crew of select individuals, including three sales and marketing leaders. Previously, those people managed the sales, canvassing, and call center teams. Now, they had to go back into the trenches and perform the jobs of their entire staffs. We couldn't go door-to-door anymore or even do in-home consultations. Instead, we had to rely on our database to call people and book appointments to sell solar systems over the phone or via video conference. Hard to imagine that we were only a week removed from high-fives, standing ovations, and gourmet pizza.

A Workforce That Refused to Quit

A few days later, the furlough letters went out. C-suite executives were not immune to the situation. Overall, we kept about eight people on staff.

My next job was to keep everyone informed of what was happening. I felt it was my responsibility to respect the people who had given me so much of their working lives over the years. I sent emails and received a variety of responses. We learned a lot about our people at that moment.

The vast majority of people I emailed were happy to hear from me and even willing to come to work, knowing they might not get paid. I witnessed first-hand how many of our team members thought from an entrepreneurial perspective. They never considered themselves to be just a cog in the wheel of our company. If they did, they would have thought, "Well, there is no wheel, so I have nowhere to go." Instead, they thought about how they could *fix* the wheel. I'm sure there are people like this in most communities and many workforces around America. However, I've never seen it as prominent as I have among the extraordinary people who live and work around the understated communities surrounding Yuba City, California. They are truly a resilient bunch.

In the following chapters, you will read the true story of the unrelenting strength of a local workforce at Westhaven Power—a hard-working, sincere, and honest group of individuals who came together in a time of near devastation to rebuild a company. Perhaps most importantly, you'll learn what grid liberation means and how it can put you in control of your own power needs while saving you exponential dollars in the short and long term. Next up, read about our real-life, real business journey and join the movement toward complete individual empowerment through Grid Liberation...

CHAPTER 1

Stop Paying the Limitation Machine

"Let freedom reign. The sun never set on so glorious a human achievement."

—Nelson Mandela (Activist and first President of South Africa)

The United States' electrical grid is one of the largest machines in the world, with a sprawling spider web of wires, poles, and power-producing equipment. Although remarkable in its scope and production, considering that its construction began in the late 1880s, it is now an outdated, overtaxed, undependable, and highly vulnerable infrastructure. Think about it: How many technologies from 1880 do you still use today? I don't see many horse-drawn carriages in driveways, nor are there a lot of telegraphs being sent or typewriters being used in the modern home.

"What hath God wrought?" If you were wondering, that was the first telegraph sent in 1844.

What do you think the inventor of the telegraph machine, Samuel Morse (also the creator of Morse code), would have thought of today's devices? Would the smartphone and the internet be considered works of the devil? Or worse, capitalism run amok?

At its worst, our current electrical grid provides a constant state of danger with millions of miles of low-hanging, high-voltage wires dangling across the countryside. These wires are ripe for picking from any storm carrying high winds or extreme weather conditions. If you're thinking, "Well, how often does something extreme happen?" The answer is several times per year, any year, in any geographic location. Tornadoes, hurricanes, excessive heat, excessive cold, and snowstorms occur regularly in various parts of the country. As the climate continues to change, they're happening with greater frequency.

At its best, the system is a limitation machine that allows us to consume power at the discretion of the public utilities. The more you use, the more you pay. Sound fair enough? Maybe, but let's take a closer look at the current realities of this system.

On the side of every building in America is an electrical meter. I call it a cash register attached by your local public utility. The meter tells them how much electricity you have used and how much you will pay for that consumption. You turn the lights on in your home, run the refrigerator, cook a meal, or even sit down for a Netflix binge, and your public utility tells you how much you owe them for the right to partake in those activities.

What if you could remove that cash register from your home? The fact is you don't need that public utility anymore.

Instead of running up a bill for every second the lights are on in your home, what if you could harness the power of a giant fusion reactor? Yes, we're talking about the sun. What if you could store that energy and never have to pay the public electrical provider one more penny? Good news, you can!

The potential of solar energy isn't what it used to be. Recent technological advances in the industry have sparked a new movement to liberate everyone from the limitation machine that is the electric utilities.

Grid liberation means we have the choice to live freely on our terms because we make all our own electricity that we would ever need. We no longer need an authority, a jurisdiction, a political party, or anyone else to tell us how much power we can use and what price we'll pay for it. We can be liberated from power outages, restrictions, and high costs.

A Book for American Consumers and Solar Providers

In the following chapters, we'll dive into more about the supreme viability of solar as a total energy solution. I'll detail the difference between *grid tied* solar energy and *grid liberation*. The latter is the way of the future, and it is how we can remove our obligation to pay a public utility for electricity usage until the end of time.

For the person who craves knowledge of emerging technologies, you'll learn the basics of solar energy and what it can do for you. You'll also learn about recent revelations in the solar industry that have made it easy to reduce your usage of the electrical grid to a mere backup system.

For solar company providers, I'll provide a call to action on how to promote grid liberation in your business. First, Yuba City. Then, the world.

In the closing chapters, you'll learn the telltale signs of a disreputable solar company. As is the case in any industry, buyers should definitely beware. However, after reading this, homeowners and business owners will know exactly what to look for when choosing a solar provider.

Before we get to any of those ideas and realizations, you need to understand who I am and how I got to leading America's charge toward grid liberation. After all, you will not blindly follow someone with a well-intended message and no practical knowledge. Rest assured that you've come to the right place, as I have a progressive history and comprehensive expertise in solar power.

My Journey to Becoming a Solar Pioneer

The first thing to know about me is that I'm not just a talking suit. I am the CEO of Westhaven Power, but I can also walk into any home or business and install a fully operational solar system.

I began my path to the solar industry by attending mechanical art school to study Heating, Ventilation, and Air Conditioning (HVAC) systems in the late 1990s. As part of the curriculum, I enrolled in a class called, The Fundamentals of Solar Energy, where I received the highest score in the class. In hindsight, that was a clear sign of where my ability to impact the world would be.

Although I'm originally from California, I didn't move to Yuba City with my wife until 1998. Much of the knowledge I carried with me about the most efficient heating and cooling systems from the East Coast hadn't found its way west. That worked tremendously in my favor, as I became widely known as an expert craftsperson in the local area. For a while, I worked with an engineer from Santa Cruz on his projects related to build hydronic heating and cooling designs.

The item that separated me from all the herd of HVAC people in the area was that I was building and using an item I learned about on the East Coast. It was called the Climate Right System, and I used a 3D printer in my garage to churn them out whenever I needed them.

Soon enough, I learned the ins and outs of solar power. Finally, I put it all together — my HVAC craftsmanship, my knowledge of the emerging solar industry, and my desire to make a difference in the world as an purpose-fueled entrepreneur.

In 2011, I founded Westhaven Power. We made about $400,000 in revenue during that first year of business. Not bad for a startup, but we had a lot of growth left to explore.

In the next few years, solar energy experienced an industry boom in Northern California, and so did our company. In 2019, we generated around $30 million. That's a big jump in eight years, but it didn't happen without a lot of hard work, a never-ending dedication to best serve our customers and a workforce that could outwork anybody.

Over the last twenty years, we've installed a clean energy solution using solar panels and batteries in almost 8,000 homes and businesses. We've also won several awards for our exemplary service and quality of work.

Why Our Story Matters

Westhaven Power is the only company—that I know of—talking openly about grid liberation. We want to introduce everyone to the benefits of solar power, but also lead America into the new world, where people take control of their own power needs.

By reading more about our mission, you'll learn how easy and cost-efficient it is to become grid liberated. By using solar energy with battery storage, you can create your own power and only draw from the grid when you choose to do so. If our grid suffers a direct attack, an act of cyber espionage, another pandemic, or any other disturbance to our way of life, follow this roadmap and your power will remain uninterrupted.

Before we talk about the simple details of how to become grid liberated, I need to explain the current state of inadequacies and hazards associated with our country's electrical grid and the many reasons to minimize your dependency on it.

The next chapter discusses how power presently gets to millions of homes across the country. Our electrical grid was an achievement by a hard-working American workforce over a hundred years ago.

However, our power needs for today have grown immeasurably since the grid's inception. We have millions of internet connections to account, heating and air conditioning systems, numerous household appliances in every home, several handheld and portable devices that need to be charged, and electrical vehicles that are soon to expand exponentially in usage. Fortunately, a safer, cleaner, more efficient, and technologically superior method has evolved.

People with a Dogged Determination to do the Right Thing

The story of Westhaven Power would not be complete without mentioning *all* of its team members. One of them wandered onto the property of our old office several years ago. He was in pretty rough shape, disheveled at best. His hair was a mess, and to be honest, he smelled a little funny. It looked like he hadn't bathed in weeks, but more than anything, he needed water and a good meal.

I'm not talking about an unfortunate soul walking the streets of Yuba City. The guy that aimlessly found our property that day was a stray pit bull. The poor guy looked like he had been through Hell and back. When I say his hair was a mess, I mean a lot of it was missing. He had patches of skin showing where the hair was removed through some inhumane act or disease.

My operations manager took the dog in because that's a typical reaction from the people who live and work in the Yuba City area; they're kind and compassionate; they want to do the right thing, not because it makes them look good, but because it's in their DNA. These folks don't turn their back on anyone, whether they have two legs or four.

It turned out that the entire workforce began looking after the dog. Several of my team members cared for him, giving him food and water every day, as well as more than enough hugs, pats on the head, and several affirmational variations of "Who's a good boy?!"

One minute with this dog, and people couldn't help but become attached. Although he had obviously suffered severe abuse and neglect, his nature was to love and be loved. However, there are legal things for any business owner to consider when having a dog on the property, especially particularly breeds, of which a pit bull is definitely one. Their dilemma with the dog was how I would react to a pit bull on the property. You'll find out more about this dog's story at the end of the book, including my reaction and where the dog ultimately landed.

CHAPTER 2

Money for Nothin': What the Public Utilities Don't Want You to Know

"You never change things by fighting the existing reality. To change something, build a new model that makes the existing model obsolete."

—Buckminster Fuller (American architect, systems theorist, designer, inventor, philosopher, and futurist.)

Many of us—at some point in our lives—have owned a car ten or twelve years past its prime with about 150,000 miles on it. The exterior has a ding or two, and it's starting to show a little rust. Inside, the passenger seat has a big rip down the middle with frays of fabric scattering left and right. Mechanically, the brakes have been a little soft for months and the exhaust has just enough duct tape applied to hold it together for its annual state inspection. Those are all things with which we can live. Bottom line: there is no problem as long as the car continues to get you from Point A to Point B reliably and without interruption.

A dilemma surfaces when critical parts break down or the leaks become too big to patch. Over time, that car will cost several hundred or even thousands of dollars every six to ten months just to patch, tweak, and replace whatever needs fixing. Each time a major part fails, our ability to get from one place to another is interrupted.

The car is no longer reliable and our ability to do what we want when we want to do it becomes impaired. At that point, we could keep pumping money into an old machine that served us well in its day but is no longer a viable long-term option, or, we could buy a new car—one with heated seats, power windows, safety technology, and much more. Most importantly, it will get us where we need to go every time without fail.

Our current electrical grid is that beat-up old jalopy. It served us remarkably well for several decades, but now, it's nickel and diming us to death, and that's only the beginning of its problems.

We're throwing money into broken-down equipment via rate hikes from the public utilities, and we're still losing service when various parts inevitably fail. The problem is only worsening because we're applying exponentially more demand on the old boy as time and technology move on.

Luckily, we don't *need* to keep pouring money into that old tin can. A shiny, new car is available, affordable, and ready to run with state-of-the-art performance. But the electric companies don't want us to realize how easy and cost-effective that transition is.

Nothing will change if American consumers keep doing what they've always done. But there are consequences with that; some of them are quite severe. The public utilities don't want us to understand the dark (pardon the pun) realities of the current electrical grid.

Increasing Demand on an Overwhelmed System

Just like that beat-up old car wasn't built to support a backup camera, blind spot sensors, or Apple CarPlay, our electrical grid wasn't built to withstand the demand for the plethora of today's modern conveniences.

A hundred years ago, the grid mostly needed to power a few light bulbs in each home. Twenty years later, we added refrigerators, radios, and televisions to our demand for power. Those old ice blocks to keep food cold just weren't cutting it.

In another twenty years, we added dishwashers and microwaves. Say goodbye to soapy hands and waiting forty-five minutes to heat a frozen dinner.

Jump ahead a couple more decades and we added personal computers and gaming consoles, among other technological advances. For better or worse, our infatuation with computing took off with these innovations.

Then, the internet happened. Game changer! Now, we have laptops, tablets, and smartphones. Once again, arguments can be made for and against these as they infiltrate the entirety of our society. Everything in moderation seems to make the most sense when exploring the evolution of technology. We'll discover this even more when the ability to escape into Augmented Reality (AR) and Virtual Reality (VR) becomes a bigger part of our lives.

All these devices, from refrigerators to virtual reality headsets, require electricity. If we fast-forward twenty years from now, we'll ask the same grid to power electric vehicles.

Not yet sold on the inevitability of electric vehicles? At the time of this writing, there is a proposal from California lawmakers to ban gas-powered vehicles in 2035. Sure, California tends to operate ahead of the curve on environmental and sustainability issues, but other states are sure to follow.

Our dependence on fossil fuels is being diminished even in states with numerous coal mining facilities. Everyone is transitioning to cleaner, safer, more sustainable forms of energy. This is a great victory for our environment, and I'm 100 percent behind it. However, we need to think about the increased demand on the grid and how to properly prepare for the future.

The average electric car consumes about two and a half times the power of the average home on a yearly basis. Our grid simply doesn't have the bandwidth to support it. We must use alternative energy to provide for this more sustainable form of transportation.

A Downgrade Disguised as an Upgrade

Our ability to generate electricity is a fundamental force driving the usage of data around the world. Any interruption to our power supply is a major disruption to our way of life. Yet, the public utilities have a strange way of solving this problem. Rather than upgrade their technology (which they try to do, but it's like putting a modern computer processor into a PC from 1995), they ask everyone to downgrade their usage at peak hours. What? For instance, California has the *Energy Upgrade* program, which tells its residents not to do laundry between the hours of 4:00 pm and 9:00 pm. Does this sound like an *upgrade?* The program promotes energy savings but seems more like a downgrade of service.

Inventions like modern heating and air conditioning, washing machines, and the internet came about because they served a purpose. They made us more comfortable, made our lives easier, and allowed us to gain knowledge more easily. Are those bad things? Of course not. Do we need to diminish our use of them? Again, no. We can use all these things without fear of damaging our environment or running out of energy. We just can't do it with our outdated electrical grid.

Does it not seem profoundly un-American for a public utility to control how much we can consume of anything? That's exactly what the public utilities do when they regulate our energy usage. They tell us that we need to conserve output of their fragile grid system or suffer periodic power outages or long-lasting downtime.

While investments in non-renewables and conservation is a good thing to reduce waste, provide cleaner air, and reduce the risk of running out of essentials like food and water, we still have the right to consume as much electricity as we need and there is no reason to do otherwise.

If we didn't have a better alternative, coddling the grid with diminished usage would be necessary. But that's not the truth with which we are operating today. Solar energy can give us all the power we need to live and work in a way that could grow the evolution of our species faster than ever. How much of an impact would Jeff Bezos, Bill Gates, and Steve Jobs had on the world if they didn't have power? We need as much power as we can harness. As a result, we need to understand the limitation machine that is our electrical grid.

- The system by which public utilities get power to our homes is inefficient, accounting for about a 35-50 percent loss by the time it reaches its destination. Guess who pays for that inefficiency? It's itemized on your electricity bill. Some of us will even notice the added pleasure of paying for a *decommissioning* fee, which accounts for a certain public utility's attempt to build a nuclear power plant on a fault line in the 1970s. Talk about money for nothin'!

- To be fair, most public utilities are planning or taking action to upgrade their system. Bravo! Now the bad news: naturally, this upgrade comes with a colossal cost attached. See the previous bullet point if you're wondering where the money will come from. Also, these upgrades are often downgrades in disguise, as is the situation with the California Energy Upgrade program mentioned earlier.

- Every public utility in the nation has proven to be negligent in a way that has created at least one catastrophic error, resulting in massive destruction.

Perhaps the most critical reason to break free of the public utilities' stranglehold on our electricity needs is the danger factor. The story of tragic circumstances due to their negligence must be told.

The Public Utility-Related Death Toll Is Rising

Negligence from the public utilities is often misstated in the media as a cost of doing business. It is not, however, a necessary evil. When analyzing safety in our grid system, many companies have chosen to save money over enhancing safety on multiple occasions.

In plain English, negligence means somebody understood the necessity to rectify or prevent the current circumstances from causing an increased risk of personal injury or damage to property and chose not to take action.

How does this happen in relation to the public utilities? Let's consider the fragility of the machine. The electrical grid is a spider web of wires running from one gangly and unsightly wooden pole to another across the countryside. In comparison, the idea of opposing wind farms because of their appearance seems ridiculous. What is more visually unappealing: a few larger-than-life windmills strategically located to provide clean power, or 150 million poles (not an exaggeration) strung together by several high voltage cables?[1]

Wooden poles are highly susceptible to deterioration and harsh weather. High winds, lightning strikes, and simple wear and tear contribute to the instability of these old-fashioned elements of the current grid system. When the poles fall due to one of those regular occurrences, high voltage wires lay on the ground and present a clear and present danger.

A hundred years ago, when we used horses to travel and mostly grew our own food, wood was the best choice to build these poles because it was the most accessible building material. Today, using wooden telephone poles and enough wire to wrap around the sun 15,000 times (not an actual fact) is inefficient at best and deadly at its worst.

If a fallen utility pole happens to be in a forested area, catastrophe is almost sure to follow, as fire can easily ignite and spread throughout the woods, destroying communities, killing wildlife, and posing an immediate threat to human safety. Sadly, this is not an uncommon occurrence.

Every public utility in America is responsible for some form of negligence based on the fragility of its infrastructure. One of the country's largest public utilities has been responsible for more than 1,500 forest fires over the last ten years. They have burned alive

---

[1] Kelly, John, "Utility Futility: Answer Man Explores the Wild World of Utility Pole Numbers," www.washingtonpost.com, September 26, 2020

more than a third of their state's wildlife and been the catalyst for many human casualties. In 2019, the company plead guilty to eighty-four counts of manslaughter. People have burned to death in their own homes due to the negligence of this company.

Fortunately for that particular public utility, the pandemic stole the headlines of what should have been a public relations nightmare for them. Right around the same time of their guilty plea, Americans' attention became consumed with news of COVID-19.

Who's to Blame?

The hard working people who built our electric grid created one of the biggest machines in the world, perhaps *the* biggest. As it grew, however, it became too big to effectively monitor and control.

There is not a singular person to blame for the hazardous nature of the grid. No one executive is responsible for the rising costs, the inefficiencies, the vulnerability, or anything else. Rather, we have an infrastructure where large teams and groups of decision makers didn't always make the best choices. In a smaller system, a few non-ideal decisions don't amount to much, but regarding something as massive as our electric grid, the smallest direction can have large-scale consequences. As a result, seemingly minor and inconsequential decisions were made to favor budgets over safety. When this happens one time, it might go by unnoticed. Several times and maybe a minor incident or two occurs. When decisions like this are made repeatedly over decades, the effect is cumulative and disaster occurs more than once. That is what every public utility is dealing with today—the effects of many shortsighted, poor choices made many times over many years.

Pivoting Our Priorities

The public utilities don't want you to know the threat their money-making machine poses; they also don't want us to know about the extreme inefficiency with which they operate; nor do they want us to understand that there is a better alternative to their outdated and overwhelmed service. As a country, we need to pivot our priorities toward a safer, healthier community.

Because America was one of the first developing nations, our grid needs a massive overhaul. As technology has increased, our way of life has evolved. Modern society has become dependent on electricity. We need power to work, play, and learn. This is how electricity is becoming the currency of the modern world.

Millions of Americans continue to get distracted and even obsess over their savings accounts and investment portfolios, living and dying with each inkling of a bull or bear market to indicate a prosperous financial future or monetary ruin.

The most disheartening part of that situation is that none of us have any control over it. Those who think they do often play the role of the fool in a game of high-stakes poker called the "free market." Those who actually do often wind up serving federal prison time, as short-selling and insider information are indeed illegal activities.

Truthfully, the overwhelming majority of investors have no way of influencing the market to move in either direction and that's how it should be. This begs the question, why bother?

History tells us that the performance of stocks, bonds, and mutual funds will rise and fall with changing political environments, global economic trends, labor developments, and many other impossible-to-anticipate variables.

This begs a follow-up question, why not transfer that time wasted on a system we can't predict to one we *can*? Solar power is the ticket to financial independence as our future becomes increasingly dependent on the reliability, affordability, efficiency, and safety of our energy resources.

For many years, people dismissed solar for various reasons. The technology, however, has come a long way. If you think you know solar, you might be surprised to discover the impactful industry changes over the last decade or two.

CHAPTER 3

The Evolution of Solar Power

"We are like tenant farmers chopping down the fence around our house for fuel when we should be using Nature's inexhaustible sources of energy —sun, wind, and tide.... I'd put my money on the sun and solar energy. What a source of power! I hope we don't have to wait until oil and coal run out before we tackle that."

—Thomas Edison (American inventor and businessperson)

All of the energy we use today is the result of capturing energy from the sun. *All of it.* For example, fossil fuels result from photosynthesis, a chemical process you probably learned about in an elementary school textbook but have since forgotten its meaning. In plain English, photosynthesis is how the green pigment in plants uses sunlight to create food from carbon dioxide and water.

When layers of earth and rock slowly covered those sunlight-enriched plants, it created tremendous heat and pressure beneath the planet's surface, which formed coal. Hundreds of millions of years later, we mine the coal and extract the solar energy stored within it, creating fossil fuel.

Of course, burning fossil fuels has limitations and negative consequences for our environment. Those are two big reasons to stop using it. After all, what happens when we run out of coal? (It is not a limitless resource.) Also, what happens when we use so much coal that our environment is irreparably damaged? Why not cut out the middle man in extracting all that powerful sunlight? Nobody needs coal or anything else to capture the energy that continues to be output from the sun every day. Unlike the unsustainable energy provided by fossil fuels, solar power is a limitless resource. Also, it naturally falls to the earth from millions of miles away every day for us to bask in its presence and gather for energy.

An Eternal Energy Resource

The sun is a large nuclear fusion reactor about 1.3 million times the size of Earth. We think of the sun as setting and rising, but it's just really burning wildly in place all the time. The earth is the moving object. Our planet spins on its axis and moves in a circular pattern around the sun. That movement constantly reorients people toward and away from our eternal energy resource, providing solar power to various geographical locations on the planet within twenty-four-hour intervals.

When we stop wasting our time with the unnecessary and unnatural process of burning fossil fuels, we can turn our focus to solar power. Then, we realize there is no need to conserve energy. That might sound strange in a "woke" world of sustainability, but hear me out.

I'm 100 percent behind creating a more sustainable situation for humanity's existence on Mother Earth. Conservation has its place in the world. We *need* to conserve clean water; we *need* to be smarter about how we get our food; we *need* to stop polluting our environment with fossil fuels and other chemical processes that damage our atmosphere and create climate change. Solar power, however, eliminates the need to burn those fossil fuels. It is an infinite energy resource that causes no damage to our environment, so why wouldn't we use as much of it as we want to?

Three Things to Know about a Solar Installation

With the understanding that solar power is limitless, we need to understand the fundamentals of installing it into every home and business that wants to support the solar initiative of clean energy.

First and foremost, solar energy solutions must be designed by a company that knows how to custom fit the right system for the individual needs of every situation. Customers and providers should be aware of the following three critical items of a properly installed solar solution.

1. Determine how much power is *needed*.

2. Determine how much power is *possible*.

3. Understand that every installation should include a warranty *and* a guarantee.

The next three sections provide detailed information about each of these items to allow people new to the idea of solar installations to get up to speed and ensure the right fit for their needs.

♀For a more comprehensive look into solar solutions, go to westhavenpower.com and download my free ebook called The Solar Results Guidebook.

Know the Output *Needed*

To determine an ideal solar solution, we first need to find out how much power a building needs. "In 2020, the average annual electricity consumption for a U.S. residential utility customer was

10,715 kilowatt hours (kWh), an average of about 893 kWh per month."[2] That is just an average. Certain homes could require much more or much less. By reviewing the last twelve months of electricity bills, we can get an idea of the output needed. Chances are that the range varies greatly according to the season and climate in which a person lives. Notice what the maximum usage looks like, because that may be the point with which needs are determined.

An important thing to remember is that our demand for electricity grows alongside technological advances. As we continue to innovate, we require steadily increasing amounts of power. This is a big reason why the current electrical grid will not be a sustainable model going forward. When electric cars inevitably become our default mode of transportation, expect to see the demand for kilowatt hours double and then some, depending on what other devices are tapping into our grid for electricity at that point. Therefore, most consumers may want to consider doubling their current energy consumption to determine how much solar power they will need within the next ten years or so, as the prevalence of electric cars is a near certainty. If you expect to have a home charger to power this vehicle, as well as other newly invented devices that require power, doubling your anticipated energy output is probably a smart move.

Consumers shouldn't allow a large estimated power output scare them off. The other option is to pay double on an electricity bill. With solar power, people recoup their investment. On the electrical grid, it's similar to leasing a car, where the lessee never stops payment because they don't own the automobile. The customer

---

[2] "How Much Electricity Does an American Home Use," www.eia.gov, October 7, 2021.

owns their solar panels. Even when financed, they will still be there providing free electricity.

Knowing our energy requirements is also essential because solar companies use panels with different capabilities. Some providers may use panels that generate 250 watts per hour, while others may prefer those that produce 400. The takeaway is not to mistake the number of panels for the same value. If Company A is offering twenty panels of 250 watts per hour each, their price should be much lower than Company B if it's offering 20 panels at 400 watts per hour on each panel.

☿ *Know what the need is for power, then consider doubling it, and find out the specifications of any proposed solar solution.*

Understand the Solar Potential

Not all roofs are created equal in solar energy potential. The direction, angle, and amount of shade the roof captures will factor into how much power a roof can harness from the sun.

Ideally, a southwest-facing roof captures the most sunlight throughout the day, but creative solutions can be designed to suit almost any situation. A Light Detection and Ranging Design (LIDAR) system analysis can ensure the power any roof can generate. Even if the LIDAR analysis produces a non-ideal number, a professional solar designer and installer can find a solution that will fit a building's unique requirements. Ramping up the solar potential in any situation could be as simple as cutting down a tree or two. The bottom line is to always think creatively and work with a good provider who is dedicated to customizing the right solution for every client.

♀Ensure what the right solar solution will look like. Is the roof constructed in a way that will allow for maximum benefit, or will someone need to create an alternative design?

Read the Fine Print

The words *guarantee* and *warranty* often get confused as being synonymous; they are not. A standard clause in a solar contract is a degradation warranty, which states that your output will not deteriorate faster than a specified rate within a specified time period. That's fine. But customers also need a guarantee that states a minimum output from the beginning of their system installation.

A well-designed solar system should last a minimum of twenty-five years. With proper maintenance, they can last much longer. With a little care, the vast majority of solar customers will enjoy their limitless energy resource for the life of their homes. The panels will likely provide plenty of power for the next homeowner and other future buyers as well.

Most reputable providers will offer a *warranty* that ensures the system will last as long as it should. They will also provide a guarantee to ensure that when people turn their system on for the first time, it provides enough power to offset their electricity bill.

♀Read the fine print of every solar contract: ensure the solar solution has a warranty *and* a guarantee.

Why Isn't Solar More Widely Adopted Already?

If the answer to our emerging energy crisis is so simple and actionable, why have we not yet implemented solar power on a global scale? Although solar is increasing in popularity (One look around on a 60-minute car drive will usually reveal several solar farms and sets of panels on individual homes), we still have a long way to go.

There are a few reasons solar isn't the primary source of our energy needs, but none of them should serve as reasons to continue going down the wrong path. The following two sections explain why solar isn't the primary energy solution for this country and the world…yet.

What Is a Solar Farm?

Solar farms are large-scale solar installations where photovoltaic (PV) panels (solar panels) or other means of collecting solar energy, like concentrating solar systems, are used to harvest the sun's power. They operate as power plants, just like a natural gas power plant or other sources of energy generation that have generated electricity for consumers for the last century.

Unlike residential and commercial systems, they're decentralized and usually consist of ground-mounted solar panels installed across large areas. There are different types of large solar projects, like community solar farms and utility-scale solar farms. Some solar projects, like those built to power data centers or other large users of solar power, have solar farms built purely for their use—sometimes onsite, sometimes offsite.[3]

---

[3] "What Is a Solar Farm?", www.Renewableenergyworld.com, April 30, 2019.

The Familiarity Phenomenon

The first reason we haven't yet adopted solar as our primary energy resource is that the grid is all we know. Familiarity and comfort have always been a difficult routine to break.

In many ways, we become the products of what our parents taught us and the knowledge they handed down. The grid and its associated public utilities were given to us from previous generations. As soon as we were old enough to move away from home, we were told we had to pay our bills, one of them being for electricity.

None of our ancestors thought of how they got electricity as a choice. Therefore, neither did we. I like to call this the familiarity phenomenon. Education is the only way for solar energy to be more widely adopted.

We must spread the word about solar power. Future generations must realize that they have a choice on how to get their electricity. This is already starting to happen, but we need to push the issue. Generation Z and beyond need to realize that they cannot continue to live in their comfort zone with the public utilities, which involves unpredictability and skyrocketing prices among other inconveniences and potential disasters. Or, they can control their own power, save money, and have peace of mind with the solar industry. Once they have this knowledge in hand, solar can truly begin to replace our grid.

With solar education spread throughout America and the rest of the world, nobody will be able to blame their descendants for their reliance on a faulty grid system, because complete control with solar power wasn't a realistic expectation until recently.

Misinformation about Cost

Another reason that solar energy hasn't completely taken over the electricity companies concerns a popular misnomer that still exists around its associated cost. Most energy consumers still think of solar power as only affordable by people with a surplus of money. Twenty years ago, that may have been true. Equipment cost a lot more for the providers in those days, which made it more expensive to install. That is no longer true.

The misinformation concerning cost wasn't solely related to solar equipment. People saw their current electricity provider as the cheaper alternative. That is also no longer true.

Recent revelations in the solar industry have made the cost of its technology lower for providers, which can now be passed down to the customers (and it is). Also, the bills from public utilities have continued to steadily rise over the last fifteen to twenty years. The combination of these two factors has shattered the myth of solar being unaffordable to the average consumer. Today, solar is—by far—the most cost-effective choice consumers can make in their choice for a power provider.

Moore's Law

Moore's Law states that computing power increases exponentially every year while the associated cost of producing the associated hardware decreases by a similar amount. The same rule can be applied to solar technology.

The equipment for solar power has gotten better, which has allowed us—the providers—to harness greater amounts of the sun's limitless energy more efficiently. At the same time, the electricity bill for all public utility customers has increased steadily over the last several decades. Therefore, today's solar solutions have better technology working for them and provide an even better cost alternative to your steadily rising electricity bill.

In a weird way, the reverse of Moore's law holds true for electricity companies. Their equipment is getting older, less efficient, and more vulnerable. Meanwhile, the cost to the consumer has become much more significant. Which side of Moore's law do you want to be on?

Moving into the Mainstream and Toward Liberation

The traditional route for the adoption of any new technology is that the first 2 percent of people are considered innovators. Solar has already got those people to buy in. The next 6 percent are usually referred to as early adopters. The solar industry has already gone through that phase as well. What is leftover is 92 percent, which represents the mainstream target audience. That is where the solar industry stands today. The job of solar company providers is now to get the attention of that mainstream target audience and show them that solar power is their ticket to cost savings and energy efficiency. It is truly the currency of the new world.

Every day, more of the mainstream energy consumers understand that the economics of solar power makes sense. Continuing to pay a steadily rising electric bill no longer adds up for many people. We need to break away from that familiarity phenomenon with the public utilities that has been there for decades.

What we've described in this chapter is traditional "grid tied" solar power, meaning the panels and other elements of your solar installation are "tied" back into the electrical grid.

The traditional version of a solar installation includes a net energy metering agreement. This is a contract that states all the power collected from the solar panels will be sold back to the public utility, which then grants the homeowner credits on their electricity bill.

A well-designed solar system will usually bring that electricity bill down to zero. However, the home is still grid tied, meaning the panels, the inverter, and your meter are all connected to and dependent upon the electrical grid. In the event of a problem with the grid, the home still receives no power.

Grid tied solar power is what makes up the overwhelming majority of solar installations in the world. At least, that is the case at the time I'm writing this. Hopefully, this book can change that. The phrase "grid tied" means the solar panels are tied into the electrical grid.

Most industry leaders are satisfied with tying their solar solution into the grid, which does a great job of saving the consumer money but does nothing to break us free from the vulnerable, inefficient, and downright dangerous infrastructure.

The sun is there; the equipment to harness its power is there; we don't need intervention from the grid to add inefficiency and vulnerability to our power supply chain. As our power demand grows with advances in technology, the currency of the new world will be energy, and it will be within your grasp to harness as much as you need. The next logical step in the evolution of solar energy is to move from "grid tied" to "grid liberated," which is a system that cuts the cord from the public utilities.

The Purpose of an Inverter

There are two types of electrical current: Alternating Current (AC), invented by Nikola Tesla and Direct Current (DC), invented by Thomas Edison. The two geniuses had a long-standing feud over which form of electricity was better for the world to adopt and implement.

Ultimately, the world settled on AC because of its ability to travel over long distances. What's interesting about this is that the sun produced DC. So one of the technological pieces of a solar solution that must be added is an inverter, which takes that DC electricity from the sun and converts it to AC solar power.

Not all inverters are the same. Varying products have ratings from much a moderate capability to much greater power potential. Think of it like the engine on a car. A typical family sedan might sport around 200 horsepower. Whereas a high-end sports car could approach 400. A ridiculously high-performance race car might get up to 600 horsepower or more. Similarly, there are inverters that will suit most basic solar installations and others that will convert enough power for a Division I college football stadium. [Sidebar end}

CHAPTER 4

Grid Tied versus Grid Liberated Solar Power

"The sun, with all those planets revolving around it and dependent on it, can still ripen a bunch of grapes as if it had nothing else in the universe to do."

—Galileo Galileo (Italian astronomer, physicist, and engineer)

An epidemic is almost certain to occur in the near future. This situation has nothing to do with COVID, Monkeypox, or any other horrible disease. Rather, it concerns a lack of resources. What happens when America's electrical grid is hacked, attacked, or overburdened by an unsustainable increase in demand? It isn't going to be pretty.

Hackers worldwide have grown increasingly sophisticated in their ability to infiltrate high-security computer systems. Physical attack, domestic or foreign, has been a threat to our society for as long as we have been on this planet. And we've already highlighted the many ways that technological advances are increasing the demand on our grid that was never made to sustain such an output. Any of these things could trigger a widespread power outage for an extended time. Unfortunately, that situation has much more dire consequences than simply being unable to watch television or browse the web. The following

A Powerless Parable

Day One of a wide-scale power outage isn't so bad. There's no Netflix to binge-watch and no video games to play, but the food in the refrigerator is good for around seven hours without power. The water pump, however, will be shut off immediately. That poses a bit of a problem, but as long as the power comes back relatively soon, crisis is averted.

Portable generators will work for a while, but they need gas, and the pumps at the gas stations won't be working. If you have a whole house generator that will work until the natural gas company can't supply their product any longer because their systems run on the grid just like everybody else's.

A populous without power for forty-eight hours goes from feeling inconvenienced to frustrated, angry, and a touch panic-stricken. Those who live in colder climates aren't getting heat. After a full day or two in sub-freezing temperatures with no heat, people will be struggling to stay warm. As bad as that sounds, it might be worse to live in a hot weather climate. At least people who live in colder climates can use blankets. Of course, blankets can only help so much if the temperature drops really low. But what happens in Arizona when the heat gets over 110 degrees Fahrenheit and the air conditioning isn't working?

The third day of a power outage is when people start planning how they will survive. Some folks will be out of food at this point. Unfortunately, the grocery stores likely won't have any food left. If they do, it will likely be gone soon, as people will resort to looting all commerce areas for supplies. Good survival instincts are mandatory to get past this point without power.

After the third day of being without power, society—as we know it— starts to crumble. The health and safety of families will be in jeopardy at this point as people fight for survival. Soon, people will be forced to either defend what they have or go on the offensive to acquire what they're lacking. Chaos enters the picture, and the result is impossible to foresee accurately. Regardless, people living in areas without power for this long will be looking for a way out. The number of refugees depends on how far-reaching the power outage is. If critical components of the grid are shut down or obliterated, the blackout could be quite expansive and long-lasting. That would mean a large number of people, potentially in the hundreds of thousands seeking asylum in neighboring regions. Then one has to wonder if those nearby areas have the infrastructure and resources to support the influx of all those extra people. To play devil's advocate, what happens if nearby regions are also out of power?

It's easy to forget how dependent a modern society is on power. The way we currently get food to our tables depends on a grocery store's power to keep it all fresh. That grocery store depends on its suppliers being able to deliver the food. To do so, those suppliers need gas and likely have computer systems that must also function.

That scenario may sound like a doom and gloom prognostication worthy of a Netflix sci-fi series, but it's more realistic than most people realize. It has been said that a region enters total anarchy after fourteen days of being without power. Sadly, it might be much less than that. This begs the question: *What are we waiting for?*

Cases of governments hacking into the electrical grids of their adversaries have already been observed. For example, we know for certain that Iran had their grid hacked; the same goes for Ukraine.

That couldn't happen in the United States though, right? Wrong. The Department of Homeland Security (DHS) has already documented hundreds of occasions when Russia has hacked America's most critical infrastructure.[4] What's worse, is that most experts agree it's almost impossible to stop them from doing it. One can't help but wonder if failure to a region of our electrical grid isn't a case of, "What if?" but, "When?"

Our peace of mind in preventing such a scenario can be had when enough industry leaders, government officials, and American consumers recognize the key difference between two types of solar power, which are grid tied and grid liberated.

A *grid tied* solar system does nothing to help us in the event of a shutdown from our grid; it is literally "tied" to the grid with a series of connections networking throughout the country. A *grid liberated* solar system, however, would provide total independence from the grid. Each house and business would have its own power supply. If our country were full of grid liberated homes and businesses, it would be next to impossible to disable our power, as a targeted strike would be required on each individual building.

For a startling look at how fragile civilization is and our total dependence on electricity, check out the novel, *Blackout* by Marc Elsburg. Although it is a work of fiction, the narrative of how quickly society degrades to violence and anarchy after food, clean water, and shelter become scarce is shocking. The most frightening aspect is how plausible the procession of events appears. In fact, the events of this book have been studied and analyzed by the government of

---

[4] Kury, Theodore J., Director, University of Florida, "Russians Hacked into America's Electrical Grid. Here's Why Securing It Is Hard," www.govtech.com, July 24, 2018.

Germany. As a result of that study, many academics have agreed with the distinct likelihood that civilization—as we know it—collapses after fourteen days of being without power.

Now, should we trust the public utilities with our precious power supply? We're talking about the same companies that plead guilty to numerous counts of manslaughter due to negligence. Somehow, the words "trust" and "public utilities" don't seem to align with the reference. Does it not seem wiser to trust ourselves to become grid liberated with solar, where we control our power individually and are free to consume it anytime we want it, regardless of what happens to the grid?

How Much Energy Can We Harness?

Those familiar with Chinese philosophy are well aware of the concept of the yin yang. It represents objects and forces that are opposing in nature but provide balance to existence. It's fair to call the preceding scenario the yin in our needs for energy in the universe. Yin traditionally represents negative forces. There is also yang in this situation, which represents positivity. Our yang, when it comes to power supply, is recognizing that we have the opportunity to harness unlimited amounts of energy. In fact, many astrophysicists and power industry analysts agree that, as a civilization, we are only in our infancy when it comes to our ability to harness energy.

"Experts assert that, as a civilization grows larger and becomes more advanced, its energy demands will increase rapidly due to its population growth and the energy requirements of its various machines. With this in mind, a scale was developed as a way of measuring a civilization's technological advancement based upon how much usable energy it has at its disposal."[5]

NIkolai Krdashev was a Russian astrophysicist who spent most of his life looking for signs of civilization from other planets. While doing so, he figured that we would be able to judge the intelligence and capabilities of other life forms by understanding how much energy they could harness. So, he created the Kardashev scale to rate galactic civilizations based on their technological ability to collect energy. Kardashev's scale describes three types of galactic civilizations: Type I, Type II, and Type III.

"Where does humanity rate on this scale?" You might be asking. It's a good question with a simple answer—we don't. As a civilization, we are not yet technologically advanced enough to register on the Kardashev scale. We are energy-harnessing infants. For this reason, most astrophysicists refer to humanity as a Type 0 civilization. We haven't even tapped the full potential of our planet's resources yet.

Before dismissing his idea as absurd due to humanity not registering on the scale, think about the infinite nature of space and time. Every star in the sky has the makings of a sun and a solar system. Some of those stars are billions of years old. By the time we see those stars in the sky, they could be completely burnt out, meaning if there were civilizations there, they may no longer exist. That doesn't mean they weren't more technologically advanced a billion years ago than we are today. That also doesn't mean we won't someday pass them in our abilities. Most scientists agree that we are about 100 years away

---

[5] Creighton, Jolene, "The Kardashev Scale - Type I, II, III, IV, & V Civilization," www.Futurism.com, July 19, 2014

from reaching Type I civilization status on the Kardashev scale. Now let's dive into what that means.

Type I indicates that a civilization is able to collect all energy from its own planet to meet the demands of its population as it grows. This includes harnessing all the energy we can from the sun.

Type II civilizations are able to control not only the energy coming *to* their planet, like the solar energy we get from the sun, but also the energy that radiates *from* the planet. To do this, the civilization would hypothetically develop a Dyson Sphere (proposed by American physicist, Freeman Dyson (not the vacuum cleaner person) or a system of orbiting solar power satellites to capture all of a planet's energy output.

Type III civilizations would also use a Dyson Sphere type of technology, but they would be able to apply it to all the stars in one or more galaxies. It is believed that this type of civilization would have access to so much energy, it would be capable of transcending the human species.

The Kardashev scale is meant for scientists to examine, explore, and experiment with. For our purposes, it's only meant to highlight the massive growth we have left as a species to harness energy. Fossil fuels will someday be considered a relic of our primitive ancestry. With that in mind, it is time for us to learn everything we can about solar energy. From there, we can begin to harness everything on our planet for more energy, more technology, and more advancement in our civilization.

When researching the Kardashev scale, most search engines will return add-ons to the three types of civilizations that were created by scientists (and amateurs) later. It is interesting to note that some people have taken the renowned scientist's theory to proclaim that a civilization can reach the level of becoming God at type VIII. However, those additional types are pure conjecture and not worthy of consideration.

Become Your Own Type I Civilization

Let's now consider how we can apply the theory proposed by esteemed scientist, Nikolai Kardashev on a much smaller scale.

Look at the countryside of American homes, office buildings, and other developments. There are clearly defined property lines in just about every situation. Within each of the property lines, there is a certain amount of solar energy that naturally falls upon every site. In a vacuum, approximately 99 percent of the homes in America would be considered a Type 0 civilization. That is if we were rating them on the Kardashev scale as if their home represented an entire civilization.

The Type 0 civilization homes consist of everyone who depends on a public utility to supply their power *and* those with a grid-tied solar solution. The only places in the world that are harnessing all the energy they can are those that create their own energy from the limitless resource that shines within their property lines daily. These people are grid liberated and can be considered a type I civilization.

A typical suburban plot size is around one-third of an acre of land. With this amount of land, a homeowner will receive about 2 million kilowatt hours per year free from the sun. Most people use around 12,000 to 15,000 kilowatt hours of electricity. Therefore, each homeowner needs to harvest only a tiny fraction of solar energy to become grid liberated.

It's now time to discover how everyone can become grid liberated.

Failsafe Power On-Demand

Although grid tied solar energy frees the American consumer from rising electricity bills, it does not liberate them from the grid. To take the public utility out of the equation, a homeowner must talk to a solar installer about a system designed to operate entirely on its own.

Grid liberated solar technology has been around for decades. When a community is built in a remote area, there are two choices for providing power to the homes. One is to run a series of more wooden poles and wires to connect everyone to the grid. In some cases, this could involve several miles of added infrastructure, increasing the chances for downed wires and poles, especially considering that the nature of a remote area usually consists of a lot of forestry. The other choice is to equip those homes with grid liberated solar power.

The U.S. military has been the biggest user of grid liberated solar power for many years. If the military was entirely dependent on the grid, one well-timed and well-placed cyberattack could destroy our armed forces' ability to communicate and take action.

Knowing that the government recognizes the importance of grid liberated power, it only seems reasonable for the American consumer to want the same thing. Understanding how the fabric of our society hinges on our ability to create power, an urgency exists to shift the paradigm of how we acquire electricity.

Grid liberation means ceasing your reliance on the fragile grid and creating your own power every day. It also means doing it in a way that is more efficient and more sustainable.

💡Visit our website to get a free grid liberation report. This roadmap details everything one needs to consider—the options for batteries and generators, as well as which appliances to buy. The process is not complex, nor is it cost-prohibitive, but it is unique, and people need to be informed of the right choices.

A grid liberated solar system requires a battery, a generator, or both. There are going to be certain times of day and weather systems that will diminish the output of solar panels. When that happens, the battery will provide power until the solar panels have stored enough energy from the sun to take back control of the demand. If the battery gets low, a generator can kick in until the battery is restored or the panels have become active again.

All the major manufacturers already make equipment that will work with no wiring involved from or to the public utility. For example, Generac—an industry leader in power equipment—sells batteries and generators designed for grid liberated solar power.

The Next Industry to "Cut the Cord"

Total industry transformation—as we're talking about it—is not unprecedented. When the automobile was invented, we abandoned our horse carriages for the faster, more efficient mode of transportation that came with the car. When the refrigerator was created, we stopped having a delivery person drop off giant blocks of ice at our homes to keep food cold. The list of improvements that have changed the way we live and work goes on interminably. Two of the most recent large-scale industry changeovers of this type are landline telephones and cable television services.

From Landlines to Smartphones

Soon, landline telephone service will be a rare sighting. Some holdovers from Gen X and Baby Boomers still have these antiquated forms of communication in their homes, mostly because of the familiarity phenomenon mentioned in the previous chapter, but younger generations are almost entirely abandoning them. Landline phones were a handed down item from previous generations that may not survive the next twenty-five years.

When the cell phone first hit the consumer market, it wasn't considered a replacement device for a landline telephone. First of all, it was roughly the size of the international space station. Secondly, the service wasn't great. The network around the device had not yet been developed to a point where a majority of people would adopt its usage.

Cell phones went through a quick evolution, however. The size was greatly reduced in a relatively short period of time. Then, flip phones became popular until the smartphone was introduced a few years later. When those hit the market—most notably, the iPhone in 2007—it became the hottest thing in consumer electronics.

As the smartphone evolved, its comprehensive list of features, including email, text messaging, and internet service, as well as the ability to play thousands of songs and take pictures, became impossible for consumers to ignore.

The service providers understood that the demand for the device presented an opportunity for them to cash in, so they built massive networks to support usage and make tons of money in the process.

That combination of unbeatable features with the ability to place calls from far-away places made the smartphone a must-have device. Although dependability and a higher voice quality of traditional phone service might make it worth holding onto, it is undeniable that landline telephones have been superseded by the smartphone. The result has been droves of consumers "cutting the cord" with their landline telephone service.

From Cable Television to Streaming Providers

Cutting the cord is most often referenced when talking about cable television. Decades ago, cable providers had a monopoly in their industry. The one fairly competitive exception was satellite providers, but they had flaws that couldn't be fixed.

The satellite providers could never make a noticeable difference for the consumer. In most circumstances, satellite television was only competitive on cost. The service was questionable—at best—whenever a bad weather system arrived. Ask anyone in the northeast how well their unsightly massive metal plate on the side of their home worked when fifteen inches of snow and ice covered it or completely broke it.

Cable companies had total control over the industry until Netflix happened. At first, Netflix was a niche company that mailed DVD movies to customers. They effectively eliminated Blockbuster and any other video rental store before taking on the cable companies.

When DVDs started to become a product of yesteryear, Netflix didn't blink. They recognized the disruption to that business and pivoted to streaming services. In fact, they actually moved to that industry a little too early. When they first announced to their customer base that they were abandoning DVDs by mail order, they received a swarm of negative feedback. So they simply reinstated it to appease their customers. Not long after, however, DVDs became similar to a landline telephone. Today, Netflix subscribers must add a DVD plan (including Blu-ray, which is also mostly obsolete) to their subscription fee if they want to receive these relics of the mid 2000s. Although that option is still available, the streaming service is the money maker for Netflix.

Following Netflix's path to streaming success came Hulu, AppleTV, Amazon Prime Video, and countless others. Not only is streaming television much cheaper than the exorbitant cable television packages, it can also be customized and the quality of the programming is better in most cases.

The average consumer began to rethink paying over $100 per month in many cases for a cable television package, of which they only used five to ten channels. Instead, they preferred to pick and choose the streaming providers they used most. Even if they bought three different streaming services, the cost still added up to less than half of what they were paying the cable providers. Also, consumers couldn't take their television set and cable box with them on the train or bus. They could, however, watch their streaming content on the previously mentioned smartphone wherever they wanted.

An undeniable fact took over the consumers' mindset—streaming services were better than cable television. Once again, it was time to "cut the cord." By doing so, the American consumers saved money, and enjoyed better service as well as enhanced features.

Now is the time for electricity consumers to do the same thing. Cut the cord to public utilities, save money, save the environment, and enjoy better service with grid liberated solar power.

💡Your local solar provider may not recognize the term "grid liberation," so ask them about designing a solar system that will allow you to cut the cord from your public utility.

From Public Utilities to Cost-Saving Solar Power

As we mentioned in the previous chapter, one of the biggest reasons solar power has become a more viable option in recent years is its affordability. The technology has gotten better and cheaper for companies to buy, and the savings has been passed on to the consumer. Additionally, financing options are more readily available than ever before.

Consumers should not hesitate to finance an item that will provide savings in the long-term. Financing items like home theater systems and designer clothing is not going to provide a return on investment. It's important to realize that there is a difference between bad debt and good debt. Bad debt is a credit card gone out of control. Good debt is a mortgage, business, or electricity for a home.

Mortgages keep people living the American dream by owning a home with a white picket fence, two kids, and a dog named Sparky running around the yard. Businesses keep the economy rolling and create jobs, which allow people to buy the previously mentioned idyllic living conditions. A solar energy solution keeps people living comfortably. People need electricity, just like they need a home and a place to work. We no longer live in a society of hunters and gatherers. Today, we need the ability to turn on lights, make coffee, access the internet, drive to work, and produce. To do those things, we need electricity. The banking system is willing to loan money for everyone in America to have those things.

Financing a solar solution replaces an electric bill with one exception— the payments are usually less. Therefore, the consumer starts saving money on day one. This cannot be stated strongly enough. The argument that solar is cost prohibitive is absolutely false. Better yet, once the system is paid for, there are no more electricity bills; just unlimited power on demand.

Grid liberation isn't a novel idea aimed at tackling an energy crisis fifty years from now. It is available today. People have a choice to pay constantly rising bills from the public utility and deal with all the flaws that come with its infrastructure, or they can create their own power.

The United States is a debt-based economy, meaning financiers have welcomed the idea of loaning money to people. If we want to buy a house, car, or any other big-ticket item, we assume debt to acquire it. Financiers don't even require the elite credit scores they used to. Most solar companies will be able to get people with a 600 credit score approved for a loan to cover the cost of their total solar installation. Some banks don't even look at the debt to credit ratio any longer. This isn't meant to serve as a public service announcement to borrow money irresponsibly, but for all the hard-working Americans who pay their bills but might have a red flag or two in their credit rating, they should know that solar installation is still something they can pursue.

Take a look at www.usdebtclock.org. There, you will see in real time the constantly mounting U.S. debt. At the time I'm writing this, the figure is over $30 trillion. Sidenote: There are other interesting figures there to analyze as well. Have fun with it!

A Bridge to the Currency of the New World

A grid tied solar energy installation is a fine step in the right direction, but we need to think beyond that. Grid liberation means less reliance on a public utility; it is our bridge to tomorrow, where a world of increasing power demands awaits, along with the opportunity to use that power to its fullest potential. With electricity becoming increasingly valuable, it will truly become the currency of the new world.

💡Solar industry providers must take these words as a call to action. They need to start the conversation with their customers about what a grid liberated system looks like. The vast majority of our clients at Westhaven Power are still grid tied, but I always talk with them about cutting the cord. Better yet, I always design their systems to ensure scalability. When they begin to tire of the public utility's flaws and rate hikes, they may decide to break free from them. If they do, their solar system will be ready to make the switch instantly. I encourage other solar providers to do the same.

CHAPTER 5

Choosing a Solar Provider

"Once you get a solar panel on a roof, energy is free. Once we convert our entire electricity grid to green and renewable energy, the cost of living goes down."

—Elizabeth May (Leader of Canada's Green Party)

Everyone *wants* to sell solar.
But not everyone *should* sell solar.

The more expensive electricity gets, the easier it becomes to show savings on solar power. Professional salespeople jump at the chance to sell solar because it's a big-ticket item (usually costing around $20,000 to $50,000, depending on the location and requirements of the structure). Although that cost is easily offset by financing and the absence of an electricity bill, the commission for the salesperson is higher than what they would make in most other industries.

A problem arises when salespeople, who lack knowledge of the industry, flood the marketplace and make promises they can't keep. For example, an inexperienced solar sales representative might sell $200,000 worth of contracts in a month and figure they're on the road to Beverly Hills. What they forget is that they need to be able to execute on those contracts.

Additionally, low-skilled contractors exist in solar like they do in any other industry. Some construction people learn the basics of how to install solar systems as a way of making more money. Sure enough, a match made in consumer Hell takes place when a smarmy salesperson sells a contract to a low-skilled installer. The consumer pays the price in that scenario in more ways than one.

What all this amounts to is the most important rule of choosing a solar provider, which is:

"Be very careful when signing a deal with a solar broker."

Anytime a solar broker is involved, a predatory sales process takes place. They're not all bad, as there are no absolutes in the universe and there are exceptions to every rule. However, you should always know if you are dealing with a solar broker and what their reputation actually is before signing anything.

Truthfully, there is no need for a middleman in the solar industry. This is a niche construction business and no broker is necessary. They're only going to add cost and sell the contract to the cheapest bidder who probably won't install the system properly.

There are plenty of excellent direct solar providers. At Westhaven Power, we are one of a brotherhood of solar companies across the country. Plenty of direct-buy solar providers exist in all areas that can design and implement a solar solution that will work without disruption for twenty-five years or more.

Solar brokers have a bad habit of creating solar orphans, which is an industry term for consumers who sign a contract with a company that does a poor installation job and then goes out of business, leaving the customer with nowhere to turn if their system malfunctions.

Two Simple Tests to Determine a Trustworthy Solar Provider

All consumers should sign a deal with a direct-buy solar provider who can do everything from selling the contract to installing the entire system and even provide maintenance when necessary.

Of course, many solar brokers may try to disguise themselves as a solar provider. These companies can be uncovered with two simple tests:

1. Place a call to the service department. Tell them you need a service call and see what happens. The service should be available 24/7, as we demand from electricity providers. If a customer can't get someone to come out to their home with one phone call, that company should not be trusted.

2. Ask for an address and show up at the business. If the company is doing business out of a trailer that also sells used cars, that is also not a trustworthy partner. However, if the company has its own facility and it looks like things are relatively well organized with several people who look like they know what they're doing, that company is probably a legitimate business.

When performing a simple online search for solar providers, numerous marketing companies will populate. Some of them may be disguised as a website that reviews solar providers. When a user leaves their email or other contact information, it's going to be sold to a solar broker.

Three or more solar providers may then reach out to the user asking to provide a quote on an installation. Figured into their cost will be a marketing fee to the company operating as a review site (solar broker). Also, these providers may not be as thoroughly vetted as the review leads people to believe. Additional measures can be taken to validate the legitimacy of any solar provider.

Validate the Licenses

Any salesperson from a reputable solar provider will know the licenses they need to design and build a solar installation. They won't have to do any fact-finding. Rather, they should be able to simply rattle off the licenses necessary at a moment's notice.

Different states may require different licenses. In California, three licenses are required for the most basic solar installations.

- The C-46 Solar license
- The C-10 Electrical license
- The C-39 Roofing license

Consumers in all states should validate that the proper licenses are held by any solar provider they're considering doing business with.

Validate the Leadership

Leadership is vital to the success of any business. The intentions, messages, and actions of good leadership get passed down to the rest of the company. As a result, the workforce translates all of those things to the customer. In a solar provider, the salespeople should be forthright and informative, the technicians should be skilled and knowledgeable, and everyone else should align with the mission and values of the company.

As the leader of Westhaven Power, my strength is in my ability to get on a roof and install an entire system from start to finish. A good validation technique when choosing a solar provider is to check into the background of its leader. What is their familiarity with solar technology? Are they simply an MBA with a general business background and little knowledge of the nuances involved in solar technology? Or do they have experience in actually building solar systems?

My team and I share a mutual respect in our abilities to get the job done. As a laborer, my background has helped me to create processes for my installers and the rest of the team that make their jobs more efficient and set them up for success. I never ask them to do anything that I wouldn't be able to do myself. As a result, our people always pass down a respectful and positive experience to the customer.

Know the Right Way to Pay for Solar Power

Paying all the costs upfront or financing are the *only* methods to consider when purchasing a solar system. Some companies may offer Power Purchase Agreements (PPA) or leases, which are essentially the same thing. The problem is that those options take the tax credit away from the homeowner or business owner.

The federal government wants as many American citizens to have solar power as possible. The current tax credit (in 2022), which has been mandated for the next ten years, is 30 percent.

Additionally, most states provide incentives to go solar as well. Each state has different incentives in place, but a few common methods include more tax credits, rebates, and renewable energy certificates. States with a high number of solar incentives include California,

Texas, Minnesota, and New York. Consult the Database of State Incentives for Renewables & Efficiency for specifics.[6]

Tax credits are sizable enough to warrant special attention when choosing how to pay for a solar installation. For those who cringe at the thought of financing, remember we are a debt-based economy, and there is a big difference between good debt (electricity) and bad debt (credit cards run amok).

Most people with a mediocre—or even slightly less—credit rating will get approved for solar financing at a reasonable interest rate for about a twenty-year term. Those with stronger credit ratings will get better rates and can opt for shorter terms.

Even a solar installation financed over twenty years provides free energy after that. During the financing term, it's basically replacing your electricity bill. With these things in mind, cost is no longer an obstacle to getting a solar system in anyone's home or business.

♀Be mindful of the details in PPAs and leases, as they will usually wipe out sizeable tax credits and potential state refunds.

Ask about an Installation without the Grid

A grid liberated solar system is blackout-proof. Solar consumers and providers should be collaborating on that idea. Providers should be showing homeowners and business owners how they can diminish their use of the grid to the point where it acts almost entirely as a back-up power source.

They should be thinking about recommendations for batteries, generators, and efficient household appliances, as well as the best

---

[6] Murphy, Lauren, Contributer and Pelchen, Lexie, Editor, "Solar Tax Credit by State 2022: What You Need to Know," May 26, 2022

solar panels to place on the roof. If the customer isn't ready to take that step toward grid liberation yet, the provider should still design the system so that the customer can easily become grid liberated with their current system in place whenever they change their mind. That day may not be next year or five to ten years later, but as the demand for electricity grows, the grid will become less reliable and more expensive. Therefore, the odds of a solar customer wanting to make the switch to grid liberated will become greater as time goes on.

💡Solar company owners who want to help drive grid liberation can contact us at Westhaven Power here for our solar results system here. We can provide you with all the marketing and other information you need to help your customers discover, create, and implement a grid liberated solar system.

A Case Study in Grid Liberation

Although the overwhelming majority of solar energy consumers are still grid-tied, Westhaven Power has installed more than a handful of grid-liberated systems as well.

Whenever I promote grid liberation as a failsafe power solution, I point to an installation we did for a customer a few years ago. His original intention was to install a grid-tied system, but he also bought three large battery systems from us for backup power.

The customer had more than one building in which he needed power, and the public utilities were giving him problems interconnecting them all. That situation dragged on for a long period of time, so the customer finally said, "I'm done fighting with those people." He switched the main breaker off and let his solar panels with batteries take over the power load.

Eight months later, the public utility finally settled their bureaucratic difficulties and were able to get his system interconnected. When they did, it was simply a matter of switching the main breaker back to the on position.

That customer's foresight paid off. During those eight months, they never lost power. That was when I realized that grid liberation was possible for the American consumer. When I saw how easily that customer eliminated the public utility from their power needs, I realized that solar energy had evolved to the point where we no longer needed the electrical grid.

Solar providers should be designing systems so that customers can remove the public utility when they want to. Those who seek control of their own supply chains, including food, water, and power are leading the way, but others who are set up to cut the cord eventually will take our mission to a mainstream option.

CHAPTER 6

Taking Control of Our Essential Supply Chains

"We sail within a vast sphere, ever drifting in uncertainty, driven from end to end."

—Blaise Pascal (French physicist, inventor, and philosopher)

When we take total ownership of our electricity, a domino effect should ensue, where the ability to control other supply chains will surface, gain momentum, and take over as well.

Grid liberation is likely to be the first of the essential supply chains that the American consumer assumes independent control. In an ideal future, others like our food supply and clean water would follow. When the citizens can assume total control of their basic needs, we become a fully liberated and empowered nation. We become stronger than ever, as the government can focus on upholding the laws that keep us united as a free society.

It's easy enough to grow our own food. Although people have the familiarity phenomenon with grocery stores, we can still tend gardens. Even in an apartment, people can grow hydroponic systems to grow vegetables.

Gaining control of our food supply would be as simple as revisiting how we nourished ourselves several decades ago. Supermarkets didn't exist in the early-to-mid twentieth century. Yet, we found a way to feed our families.

Water is another basic human need. If we can collect and purify our own water as well, we have secured our basic needs without reliance on a city water system, a grocery store, or an electric company. Control over supply chains doesn't mean excommunicating ourselves from society. We can still live, work, and play in the public sector, but we won't depend on big businesses or the government for any of our basic needs.

The fear of attack from foreign countries is mainly based on a concern for our supply chains being disrupted. In the back of our minds, we're thinking, "What happens if someone attacks our supplies of food, water, or power for an extended period of time?" If we have independent control over these supply chains, that fear dissipates into nothing.

Grid liberation can be the first step we take, as a society, to take control of our supply chains.

The spread of COVID-19 provides a good example of how necessary it is to have these basic resources. Imagine the increased impact if we had to manage an extended disruption to our power at the same time.

Dealing with the pandemic was bad enough. What would have happened if we couldn't work from home? What about our kids being able to attend school remotely? What if we couldn't Facetime friends and family when we desperately needed to see a friendly face? What if we couldn't have Amazon deliver supplies to our front door?

The effects of the pandemic were harsh, but they would have been 10x harsher if we didn't have the electricity needed to connect ourselves to the outside world. Was COVID a one-time thing? Highly doubtful. Our civilization periodically deals with widespread disease as a wild card to our existence. Look up the black death and the Spanish flu. Those diseases claimed a large chunk of the planet's population. COVID wasn't the first pandemic and it won't be the last.

What's worse is that disease isn't the only thing that can take society into the dark ages. Military conflicts, economic crises, cyberattacks, and fascism will always threaten our way of life. Don't mistake my words for wild conspiracy theories. History tells us those things happen with a fair amount of regularity. What's next?

When whatever's next happens, do you want to hope the public utilities make the right decisions? Do you want to hope the grid stays intact? Or do you want to have total control over your own power needs?

💡 Take that first step toward grid liberation and enjoy the peace of mind in knowing your power will stay on if and when the grid fails. Visit our website for more information today.

Conclusion

"When I am abroad, I always make it a rule never to criticize or attack the government of my own country. I make up for lost time when I get home."

—Winston Churchill (Former Prime Minister of the United Kingdom)

As I sit in my office trying to kickstart the American movement toward grid liberation, I continue to feel immense gratitude for the people who believed in our mission throughout the COVID-19 pandemic. My team at Westhaven Power showed tremendous resilience and strength in the toughest of times. Without them, I would not be writing this book. Because of the efforts of my team members, we not only weathered the storm provided by COVID, we came out better for it.

Any business leader knows we learn our most critical lessons by surviving the most difficult challenges. I learned how great the company's people were and still are today. I also learned how to leverage creativity to solve problems that money can't. Additionally, I learned that *the U.S. government has plenty of people who want to do the right thing.* Go ahead and read that twice if needed.

Are there plenty of politicians who care about nothing other than their own personal gain? Sure. But are there plenty of others who take their jobs just as seriously as other hard-working Americans?

Absolutely. I even talked to some of them. I had to, because it took an actual act of congress to keep Westhaven Power up and running.

I realize this will cause some sneers, jeers, snickers, and even a bit of shock, but I am grateful for the government of the United States of America.

It's true. We all like to vent our frustrations about the government. After all, freedom of speech is one of the main principles instituted by our founding fathers. In America, we're allowed to say that the bipartisan politics we endure is frustrating, insufferable, and maddening. We're allowed to point fingers at certain members of Congress, the Senate, or even the President. When citizens of certain other countries try that, they tend to disappear. Not in the U.S. We let freedom ring, and I'm proud of that. I'm also proud to say that Westhaven Power would have likely never made it through COVID had Congress not passed the Paycheck Protection Program (PPP) in the middle of the outbreak in 2020.

Please don't mistake my gratitude for having rose-colored political glasses. I understand the government has failed its people on many occasions. My point is not to glorify its inconsistencies or inadequacies. Rather, I'm simply stating that our government does have times where it works, and we're not as quick to recognize those successes as we are the failures.

The PPP was a $953-billion program that loaned money through the Small Business Administration (SBA) to various businesses across the country. It covered two-and-a-half months of expenses, including payroll, utilities, rent, and a few others at a low interest rate. The program was designed to get American businesses and workers through a time of crisis. Of course, it wasn't quite that simple for us, but that was no fault of the government. In fact, congress actually saved the day by picking up the pieces after a certain large banking institution (which was bailed out with billions of dollars in the economic crisis of 2008) mishandled my PPP paperwork. The problem started with a technicality about how our employees were paid.

At Westhaven Power, we used a payroll service, which should not have been a problem. Approximately 30 percent of America is paid through a payroll service. Anyone who falls under that category, for legal purposes, is designated as a leased employee. In reality, that means nothing. All the employees at Westhaven Power were full-time workers. In bureaucratic bulls**t, it almost meant the dissolution of my business.

After filing the PPP paperwork, I was waiting on a check for a little over $1 million to cover our payroll and other expenses to keep the business afloat. Thirty days later, I was notified that our PPP loan was approved. I was ecstatic.

Getting that notification meant that all the people who were furloughed, but still showing up for work every day, were going to get paid. We at Westhaven Power had a stay of execution.

I raced home to get on my computer, pull up the e-documents, and sign the check. During that ride home, I called a bunch of people to let them know that we got the loan and they would be paid as soon as I could cash the check. When I got home, I pulled up the email, clicked the document that showed how much the check was for, and saw it was written for $37,000.

My eyes did that thing where they kept staring at the number, thinking that it was an illusion of some kind. "Maybe there's another check somewhere in the paperwork?" I thought. I doubled and triple checked everything. The amount was almost $1 million shy of what we needed.

The problem was that our bank didn't acknowledge any of the leased employees in my company. So, the PPP paid out the exact amount of all the non-leased employees at Westhaven Power, which was me.

Of course, all bad news comes after 5:00 on a Friday, so our bank was shut down and I couldn't get any answers that night. Fortunately, a weird circumstance worked in our favor. We had brought in a local yoga studio as a partner about a year earlier. One of the studio owners had contacted me about three weeks earlier in a state of panic. She didn't know what to do to keep their business alive. So, I told her about the PPP and she was delighted. They filled out the paperwork and her bank handled everything perfectly. The yoga studio got the money and was able to survive the pandemic.

I thought about her situation and wondered if her bank might be able to help us as well. So, I called her and asked what bank she used. She told me they got their PPP done through one of her yoga studio members, who was the President of a small, local bank. I asked her for his number and left a message on his voicemail asking for help.

A couple of hours later, my phone rang. It was the President of that local bank. He gave my information to his chief loan officer, who started working with me immediately.

I didn't tell anyone else at the company, but we were running on fumes at the time. All of our vendors were overextended, and there wasn't any money left to stay in business. I was on the phone all day, every day with the SBA, trying to secure our PPP, telling them that our bank was at fault and they weren't going to help me. That part might be the most infuriating. I called that original bank of ours a hundred times, probably. Toward the end of the calls, they admitted they made an error, but also told me there was no way they could correct it. At least, they weren't going to take the extraordinary steps required to fix it. The only thing they were good at was the way they tried to calmly explain how they screwed up and weren't going to help me take the issue any further. They were quite polite when telling me that they were basically putting me out of business.

Finally, I decided to call my local representative. I was as shocked as anyone when someone actually picked up the phone and spoke to me. The congressperson's name was John Garamendi. In the eleventh hour, he got our second attempt at our PPP loan pushed through. Few people can say they instigated an act of congress; I'm proud to be one of them. I'm even prouder to be a citizen of a country where something like that is possible. The U.S. government worked with a small, local bank and saved Westhaven Power.

For the next several months, many of us worked seven days a week, trying to keep the company afloat. The PPP enabled us to pay everybody who kept their faith in the company's ability to weather the storm, continue to provide solar power, and keep the message of grid liberation alive.

Today, Westhaven Power is back in the saddle, employing about eighty people and bringing solar power to people's homes and businesses all over the local area. We're profitable and spreading the message of grid liberation louder and clearer than ever. In fact, it might be time to clear out our celebration room again. Maybe we should open it to the public as a grid liberation announcement?

Epilogue

"Dogs and philosophers do the greatest good but get the fewest rewards."

—Diogenes (Greek philosopher)

Wondering what happened to the pit bull that wandered onto our property several years ago?

When I found out about the dog, I couldn't help but fall in love with him. He was such a gentle beast. All he wanted was the company of some good people, which we had in abundance at our company.

We decided to call the dog, Haven. Of course, he couldn't just continue wandering on and off the property for food, water, and attention. So, we had to figure out the best thing for Haven going forward.

The team got together and decided that Haven could serve two roles for the company: chief security officer and mascot. It didn't matter that Haven would back down from a flea with an anger management problem. The imposing nature of his breed and the sheer muscle he gained since we started feeding him were plenty to ward off any burglars or others with malicious intentions.

As far as the mascot goes, Haven adapted to that role without trying. Everybody loved him, so he became the face we all wanted to see when times were tough. There's nothing quite like looking into the unconditionally loving eyes of a dog when one needs a pickup.

My family and I adopted Haven. We got him to a veterinarian who gave him all his shots, started feeding him the best dog food we could find, and gave him a warm bed to sleep in every night. Of course, he still has to fulfill his duties at work during the day, so I take him to work with me every morning.

Near bankruptcy, plague, and anything else the world can throw at us will be met with the positive attitude of this beautiful creature, who will provide us with all the love and support we need.

The bottom line: Haven ended up in a good place and so did our company. Now, if we can just get grid liberation promoted throughout the Yuba City area, the country, and the world, we'll all be in a better place.

Acknowledgements

I would like to acknowledge the entire staff at Westhaven Power for all their care and support during every kind of trying time imaginable. They have taught me the value of resilience and persistence and that it always pays off. I would not be where I am today without all of their dedication and purpose driven actions.

About the Author

Brett Joerger is the Chief Executive Officer (CEO) of Westhaven Power. He grew up in Southern California with his mother, who always reminded him to be humble, grateful, and honor the people around him. He has taken those words to heart as an adult and a businessperson.

Throughout his twenty-plus years of experience in the solar industry, Brett has become a master craftsman and a dedicated leader. He is always quick to point out the invaluable contributions of everyone in his company as the key to the success of his business.

At Westhaven Power, Brett advises his customers not *only* to go solar, but to become *grid liberated.* Through his extensive experience and industry knowledge, Brett tells people how to take control of their own power by installing systems that can remove them from dependence on the vulnerable and overworked infrastructure of the public utilities. Follow Brett on LinkedIn or Twitter. Better yet, join his cause to become grid liberated:

www.ingramcontent.com/pod-product-compliance
Lightning Source LLC
Chambersburg PA
CBHW070446130626
46553CB00006B/2301